old dog town

old dog town

michael mountain

GIBBS·SMITH
PUBLISHER

SALT LAKE CITY

First Edition

05 04 03 02 01   5 4 3 2 1

Published by
Gibbs Smith, Publisher
P.O. Box 667
Layton, UT 84041

Orders: (1-800) 748-5439
www.gibbs-smith.com

Designed by Dawn DeVries Sokol
Edited by Gail Yngve

Library of Congress Cataloging-in-Publication Data
Mountain, Michael.
Old Dogtown/Michael Mountain. —1st ed.
p.cm.
ISBN 1-58685-110-1
1. Dogs—Utah—Kanab—Anecdotes. 2. Animal rescue—Utah—
Kanab—Anecdotes. 3. Dogtown (Animal sanctuary) I. Title.
SF426.2.M68 2001
636.7'0832'0979251—dc21
2001003407

contents

Dogtown
at Best Friends

As soon as we at Best Friends began Best Friends Animal Sanctuary in the mid-1980s, we noticed how the dogs tended to build their own society, establish their own rules and codes of behavior, take on their own jobs, and form themselves into a town that was not too different from the communities in which we humans live. The stories in this book are all true. All I have done is "translate" their language into ours, in order to convey some sense of the inner life of Dogtown.

Old Dogtown is about the older dogs at Dogtown—in particular those who, like Ginger, Amra, and Higgins, were here pretty much from the start. In their own way, they built Dogtown. And the success of Best Friends is really their success. It's nice to know that a group of unwanted, abused, and neglected dogs have created their own society, their own legends, and their own mythology.

Their story is also part of a larger story. At the time Best Friends was beginning, seventeen million homeless dogs and cats were being destroyed in shelters across the United States each year. Today, that figure is below five million and still dropping as the No More Homeless Pets movement grows.

Thousands of kind and caring people across the country make the work of Best Friends possible through their donations to the sanctuary. Many of them also visit the sanctuary each year and work alongside the staff to help the dogs and cats and other animals get ready for good new homes. On any given day, there are about 750 dogs at the sanctuary. Some are here only for a few days or weeks—others for much longer. Either way, thanks to you, their new life is one that truly makes up for everything that went before.

Thank you all for making it possible. You can keep up to date with the latest news from Dogtown, and all the other areas of the sanctuary, on the Best Friends Web site at www.bestfriends.org.

And now, let's turn this over to the dogs!

—Michael Mountain

How Ginger
Helped the Federal Reserve Tree Grow Tall and Green

Ginger sat down under the Federal Reserve Tree and decided to count the tennis balls.

She didn't really *have* to count them but she liked to do it anyway—just once in a while. And today was the perfect day. The summer rains had given way to bright blue skies over Dogtown, and she found herself remembering that beautiful morning when she first woke up at the sanctuary.

Counting the tennis balls always brought pictures and scents of the old days back into her head—her first night at Dogtown, meeting Sheriff Amra the Malamute, Victor the Dogfather, and all the other Golden Oldies. She also remembered how far they'd all come over the years and how many new dogs now came from far and wide looking to start a new life at the Best Friends Animal Sanctuary just as she had done thirteen years ago.

Yes, today was a perfect day to count the tennis balls again. . . .

Ginger.

Welcome
to Dogtown

Thirteen years earlier . . .

Ginger had been liberated from a puppy mill by the police. She'd lived—if you could call it living—in a tiny cramped pen, forced endlessly to breed more Chesapeake Bay retrievers to sell to bird hunters. One evening, there had been a terrible commotion, ending with the owner brandishing a gun at his wife and children. Then, the police arrived and took him away, and then some people from Best Friends came to collect Ginger and thirteen other dogs, including her two pups, who were already being used for breeding.

It was well after midnight when they arrived back at Best Friends. The first thing Ginger could see as she got out of the truck was that there were no cages or tiny pens anywhere in sight. Just the big blue sky, lots of dogs and people, and Sheriff Amra, who had been snoozing outside Octagon Two (or Daisy Mae's Saloon as most of the dogs called it), harrumphing up to her, checking her out as a possible trafficker in contraband biscuits, and then sniffing his friendly welcome to her and the other new arrivals.

Sheriff Amra had been snoozing outside Daisy Mae's Saloon.

Ginger and her pups settled down under a tree and two of the people brought over a nice doghouse and told her they were naming this area the Chesapeake Bay in honor of her being a Chesapeake. Ten minutes later, they were back with a midnight snack. It was a bigger meal than Ginger had ever had back at the puppy mill, so she didn't mind Sheriff Amra "tasting" it first. Afterward, she lay down for a nap and, moments later, was fast asleep.

When she woke up again, it was bright daylight. There were big homes, small homes, and fenced areas stretching as far as she could see or smell. But what had awakened her were lots of dogs with wagging tails, barking and racing around nearby. The breakfast truck was heading in her direction with the Sheriff, of course, following close behind to "monitor" the proceedings.

Ginger finished her breakfast (*"Thank you, Sheriff, but we don't need any help eating it."*) and took the pups for a stroll down to the big octagon buildings.

What a scene! Dogs running in and out and racing each other up and down the fences. People loading bowls onto trucks and driving them to dog homes that stretched up the hill. And the Sheriff nonchalantly "confiscating" an occasional bowl and taking it off to his private stash in the bushes "for further identification," as he put it.

Victor's Line in the Sand

On her way back to the Chesapeake Bay, Ginger was about to take a short cut through the trees when she was stopped by an invisible line in the sand that was marked with an unmistakable message: *Do Not Cross.*

This line had obviously been established by the creaky old dog who was carefully getting to his feet and walking slowly over to her, his legs trembling

Nobody ever crossed Victor the Dogfather's line in the sand.

slightly from arthritis. He was Victor the Dogfather, and the line in the sand was the boundary of Victorville—his very own domain—with its private militia of rowdy youngsters, all former strays and street dogs sporting missing legs, ears, and teeth as emblems of past derring-do on the back streets of nameless cities.

Ginger sat down and watched the comings and goings at Victorville. She

Ginger's pups, Cheshire and Mace.

observed that none of the dogs (not even the Sheriff) ever crossed Victor's line in the sand without permission. After a while, the Dogfather limped up to her, with his boisterous guard in tow, sniffed her over, and welcomed her to Victorville. But although the Chesapeake Bay was only two trees away from Victorville, and even though Ginger and Victor were soon to become the closest of pals and neighbors, she always respected his line in the sand and never tried to cross it uninvited.

Victor looked to Ginger like one of those dogs who carried the weight of the world around his neck. She was right. The old Dogfather had spent most of his life tied to a heavy chain in an old trailer park. He'd sat there for years, largely ignored, watching and listening to all the petty squabbles and sniffing the air to keep up with the daily mini dramas, the comings and goings, the various loves and hates. Then, one sweet day, there were fresh faces, fresh smells, release from the heavy chain, and now his very own domain: Victorville.

Life at Dogtown

After a few weeks at Dogtown, most of the dogs that had been rescued with Ginger were ready to be sent off to good new homes, but her pups, Cheshire and Mace, had some health problems, and Ginger was hardly a spring chicken herself. So the three of them settled down to make a permanent life at Dogtown.

Their life there would also mean finding a new career. A trip to the spay/neuter clinic had ensured the end of her former job of breeding endless litters of puppies for sale.

Everyone at Dogtown had a special occupation. At the clinic, Ginger had met Nurse Dusty Anna, whose main job was making sure that any dog coming out of surgery would always wake up to a nice big kiss.

Suzy, a gentle German shepherd who lived next door to the clinic, ran a kindergarten school for abandoned puppies that she watched over and taught manners to until they were ready to be adopted.

Deputy Claire patrolled the fence around Octagon One. Not that anyone was ever observed doing anything wrong on the inside of the fence. But *that*, Deputy Claire explained with the faintest curl of her lip, *was* the point. And she was going to make sure no one was ever *going* to do anything wrong.

On the remote possibility that someone *might* do something wrong,

Suzy and one of her students.

news reporter Missy the Border Collie would be sure to report it. She spent her days racing from one octagon to the next, letting everyone know what was happening. Other than the occasional theft, trespassing, or rough-and-tumble, Missy focused on the sports news, especially who'd just scored in the top-league fence game between Octagons Two and Three.

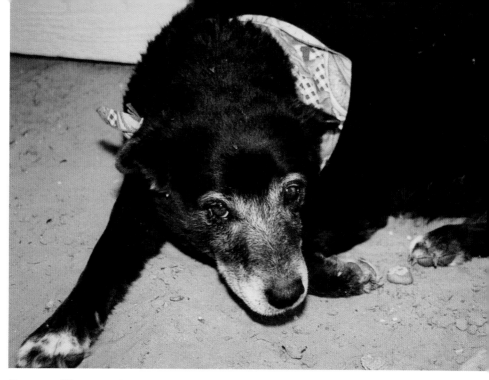

Deputy Claire relaxed after her daily patrol.

Just up the path at Octagon One, Maddie, which was short for Mad Dog (although she was clearly not mad at all—just a little intense when it came to bowls that might need cleaning), supervised kitchen operations.

All of this was presided over by the Sheriff, a giant red Malamute who had been unceremoniously abandoned at Best Friends by his former family. Someone had probably decided that he was too big for his/her home or lifestyle, so he/she had sneaked up to Dogtown in the middle of the night, left Amra at the front gate, and driven off.

Amra was doing his usual "confiscating" of the occasional bowl or biscuit for his private hoard, and greeting all visitors in the expectation of receiving a small gratuity.

Behind every great sheriff, of course, there is always a great sheriff's wife who works hard to make sure her husband never lags in the opinion polls. In Amra's case, she was a small, unassuming, brown dog who was never more than a few steps from his side. Her name was Rhonda, and she kept him company all day, every day, making sure his fur was tidy and giving him a quick kiss if he was feeling grumpy on a

Maddie supervised kitchen operations.

hot afternoon when there were visitors to greet.

All in all, there were between six and seven hundred dogs at Dogtown on any given day.

The Federal Reserve Tree

Like all dogs, retrievers have their own special skills, and it took Ginger only a few days to figure out a new career for herself and her pups that would make them an invaluable part of their new home.

Dogtown itself was only a few years old. It had sprung up virtually overnight as word got around about this new haven for abused and abandoned canines. Like other towns that spring up in the Wild West, it had become a magnet to dogs from hundreds of miles away, all seeking a new life and a rare opportunity.

As a consequence, the economy of Dogtown was becoming quite stretched. While the Great Temple of Food, a big metal building at the top of

Missy the Border Collie, Dogtown's news reporter.

Rhonda and Amra.

the hill, never actually ran dry, Dogtown was in danger of slipping into a recession when Ginger arrived. The answer to that, Ginger thought to herself, was a good retriever and a proper bank.

That afternoon, she set off across Dogtown with her pups. Just a week earlier, the town had received a big donation of tennis balls, but many of them were already lying under bushes or buried in the sand.

Over the course of the afternoon, Ginger and her team retrieved dozens of the tennis balls and brought them back to the tree next to her doghouse.

The following morning, a group of dogs showed up at her tree and, thinking Ginger wasn't looking, grabbed a tennis ball each—sometimes two—and made off with them. Ginger didn't mind. That afternoon, she simply set off with her team to collect them all up again.

Everyone soon realized that the Chesapeake Bay was *the* place to go for tennis balls. Ginger never tried to stop them. She'd just round up the tennis balls again the next afternoon and put them back under the tree—the Federal Reserve Tree, as it became known.

Keeping the tennis balls circulating kept Dogtown humming. Ginger soon added biscuits and other treats to the new currency. Her economic recovery program was quite simple: collect everything up and then share it out again. After all, if the dogs were afraid of someone taking their tennis balls away from them, they would hoard them and bury them, and then no one would have any fun. But as long as they knew there would always be a good supply, there was nothing to worry about.

It certainly seemed to work: Dogtown grew bigger, and more people sent tennis balls or came to visit—bringing more treats and goodies with them.

As the years passed, the Federal Reserve Tree grew bigger and shadier than ever.

How Mayor Jethro
Found His Golden Biscuit

It was a hot summer afternoon, and Ginger had finished her daily rounds and was snoozing contentedly under the Federal Reserve Tree, when a shaggy young dog called Jethro arrived at the front gate of Dogtown.

The happy-go-lucky outlaw had fallen in with an ornery young man—a drug dealer, no less—who was now in prison. As a young dog, he'd learned some rowdy ways himself and had eventually been arrested and hauled into court in a small dusty Arizona town. He was too unruly to be adopted, said the police officer. Everyone in court seemed to agree. No, sir, Jethro's future did not look at all bright!

But the judge was a kindly old fellow who had heard about Dogtown, and he whispered to Jethro's attorney that if the dog were to get out of town right now and never come back, the court might just turn a blind eye to the whole matter.

"Well then, old buddy," he said with a stern wink as he pointed to the open door, "you'd better get out of town, and fast! And don't let me ever see you back!"

Hitching a Ride

Jethro simply couldn't believe that someone had finally given him a chance.

The happy young outlaw was hauled into court in a small, dusty Arizona town.

Lickety-split, Jethro hitched a lift aboard the first wagon headed out of town with his attorney, who was a regular volunteer at Dogtown and was headed up there anyway for a week of scooping the poop.

"Land of opportunity for fellas like you, Mr. Jethro," said the attorney. "Prospectors say there are golden biscuits there." (Jethro positively leaped into the front seat.) "Just stay on the right side of Sheriff Amra, and, why, he might even let you dig for some of them."

Welcome to *Dawgtown*!

Jethro soon found himself face to face at the gate with the Sheriff.

"Welcome to Dawgtown," said the huge Malamute, peering into Jethro's shaggy coat. "Don't happen to be hiding any contraband in all that shaggy hair of yours, do you?"

"No, siree," replied Jethro, to the evident displeasure of the Sheriff.

Jethro decided he was a mite hungry, so he saddled on over to Daisy Mae's Saloon, famous for its spring-house water and its doghouse grits. The proprietor, Daisy Mae, met him at the door.

"Howdy, pardner!" said the big, black, old Lab with droopy ears who, folks said, knew every secret of Dogtown. "You must be young Jethro. This one's on the house for newcomers."

After a good dinner, it was time to find somewhere to stay. "A fella about your size hit the jackpot yesterday and went off to live with a fine lady in California," Daisy Mae explained. "Maybe you can move in with his pals."

She gave a low growl, and a three-legged old timer came hopping over. "This'll be Shamus. He'll teach you about prospecting for golden biscuits. Not that anyone's ever found any. Take Jethro here up to Octagon Three," she ordered.

"Sure thing, Daisy Mae," said the three-legged prospector. "Yes'm, there's biscuits in them thar cupboards!" he announced, as he hopped away, followed by a puzzled Jethro.

A smiling old mutt stepped down from his porch to greet them at Octagon Three. "My name is Bernard, and I have an extra bed if you care to take it. That kind attorney of yours rented it for you. And don't pay too much heed to old Shamus," he added in a whisper. "He keeps drawing treasure maps in the sand, and he's quite certain the legendary golden biscuits are buried here at Dogtown."

Digging for Golden Biscuits

The next morning, Jethro began digging for the golden biscuits. Day after day he dug while the other dogs played.

The months passed, and then the years. And still he dug, as new dogs came and went. But he never found anything, and people began to forget he was even there.

Then, one spring morning, several years later, the big shaggy dog awoke just as the sun was rising over the canyons. He yawned and stretched, and that was when he caught sight of the golden biscuits. They weren't buried in the sand at all. They'd been in plain sight every morning—those golden red canyons that surrounded Dogtown, illuminated by the magical early morning sunlight.

And that was when the light had dawned on him, too, and he sat for a while, gazing at all the treasure that was around him. Today there would be

"Thanks, old pal," whispered Jethro (right) to Bernard.

no more digging: He would look up instead of down as he set off on a jaunty walk around Dogtown.

He nodded to Ginger as he passed the Federal Reserve Tree. The old Chesapeake had always been kind to Jethro and encouraged him in his search.

He watched as Bernard, his roommate, tried to hitch a ride with every pretty girl who was visiting the sanctuary. *(Gotta find Bernard a home, he thought to himself.)*

And he stepped aside as Missy the Border collie raced (well, it was more of a trot these days) up and down the fences telling the other dogs the morning news. "Found your golden biscuits yet, Ol' Jethro?" she asked as she ran past him. *(Ah yes, he thought to himself. But no one would ever believe me if I told them I'd really seen the golden biscuits.)*

Mayor of Dogtown

Jethro began taking over some of the late Sheriff's duties. The old Malamute had gone over the Rainbow Bridge a year or two back and was already the stuff of legend around Dogtown. One morning, when the sun was coming up, Jethro even fancied he caught a glimpse of Amra right there in those golden canyons.

Everybody missed Amra, so Jethro came to the gate of Dogtown every afternoon to greet the visitors—with Bernard often by his side. And although he had carefully buried the secret of the golden biscuits deep in his shaggy dog coat, it kept gleaming through until everybody who came to Dogtown wanted to pat him and run their fingers through his hair. One day, Bernard even proposed that Jethro become the new sheriff.

"Oh, I'm just an old outlaw," replied Jethro. "I could never take the Sheriff's place."

"Well, doggone it," said Bernard, as he saw Missy come sprinting around the corner. "I'm nominating this 'ere Jethro for *Mayor* of Dogtown, then."

Missy wasted no time spreading the news, and the next morning, there it was in the *Daily Bark*: *"Ol' Jethro becomes New Mayor of Dogtown."*

"I wish I could hang a golden biscuit around your neck," said Bernard, as his old friend was sworn in as Mayor of Dogtown.

"Thanks, old pal," whispered Jethro to his new deputy. "And don't forget to tell everyone that if they just keep looking up, one day they'll discover the secret of the golden biscuits, too."

Old Friends Are Best Friends

The Odd Couple

Today—seven years later . . .

Sebastian and Higgins spent this morning getting ready for their birthday party. For Sebastian, that meant enjoying lots of hugs from friends and visitors; for Higgins, it meant grumbling about all the unnecessary fussing around. Nobody could remember quite how old they were (the best answer was "very"), nor did anybody have any idea of their real birthdays. But Higgins came to Best Friends one August even earlier, so his birthday party had always been in August. And since this odd couple shared everything with each other, it was Sebastian's official birthday, too.

The party was going to be at Dogtown's Town Hall, and Higgins was not looking forward to it. Higgins rarely looked forward to anything that would be considered fun. Nor did he like anyone very much—except Sebastian.

For his part, Sebastian didn't just love Higgins. He loved everyone—cats, dogs, kids, trees, rocks! Meanwhile, Higgins followed him around, grumbling at everyone. (And, if no one was around, he still grumbled to Sebastian, presumably about the fact that there was no one to grumble at.)

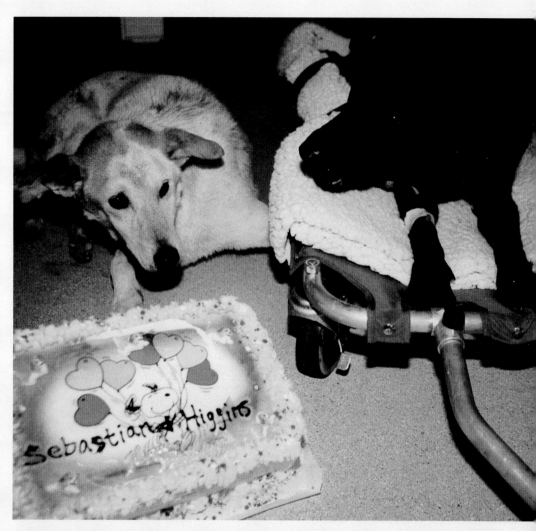

Sebastian's new cart did not please Higgins, who didn't like anything on wheels.

Orson Wells (right) was said to have worked a miracle on his girlfriend, Lady.

Hardly anybody took much notice of Higgins's grumblings. The other dogs were all used to him greeting them with a raspy growl as he tried to look his scariest by baring the few teeth he had left. As the most senior of senior citizens at Dogtown, Higgins had earned the right to be as grumpy as he wanted. In any case, Sebastian more than made up for Higgins's general demeanor by walking around with a permanent huge, wide, pink-tongued, toothy grin.

At three o'clock, a special cart arrived to give Sebastian a ride to his birthday party. A few days before the party, he'd had a small stroke, so he was still a little wobbly on his feet. The cart did not please Higgins. He didn't like anything on wheels, so he grumbled when the cart was wheeled in. He didn't like having his photo taken, either, but he enjoyed the birthday cake, said hello to Ginger, and even tolerated a hug from some of his fans. Sebastian had a whale of a time, and then it was time to go back home to Old Friends again. ("The wheels again," sighed Higgins.)

Lady and Orson Wells

On their way back to Old Friends, Sebastian wanted to stop and visit Lady and Orson Wells. These two were famous all over Dogtown since Orson was said to have worked a miracle of love on his girlfriend.

Lady and Orson Wells were rescued from the mean streets of a Los Angeles suburb—and just in the nick of time. When the two arrived at Dogtown, Lady was already coming down with paralysis in her back legs. Within a few days, she could no longer walk, and soon after that she was at the Best Friends clinic, barely able to lift her head. Worse, she'd stopped eating and seemed to be losing the will to live.

After lots of tests, nobody was quite sure what was the matter with Lady. But when Orson was brought in to visit her, Lady perked up just a little. So one of the vet staff sat down with the two dogs and told them that they would never again be separated and that if they wanted to live a long life together, then Lady should start getting better now. She looked up, a little gleam came into her eye, and, from that moment on, she did indeed begin to get better.

When she was strong enough, Lady went to a big university hospital for treatment. Orson, of course, went with her. Today, she went for a short walk again in the soft sand of Dogtown with Orson always at her side. After that, they groomed each other, sat together, shared their food, and then went into their favorite doghouse, which, like everything else in their life, was specially fitted for two.

Higgins muttered something about "all that lovey-dovey stuff," while Sebastian gave Lady and Orson one of his big smiles before heading back up the hill to Old Friends.

Old Friends

Old Friends was Dogtown's new retirement home. The focus there was less on tennis balls and golden biscuits, and more on cots and fluffies and who was going to snuggle up with whom for a nice nap.

Coyote was queen of the fluffies. She wasn't a coyote at all, but the people who brought her to the sanctuary thought she was, so that was her name. Coyote's best friend was Rose—perhaps because they're both diabetics. At any rate, Coyote loved to dig holes in the sand, and Rose loved to sleep in them.

Coyote, the queen of the fluffies.

Sargeant, Gina and Sampson all shared the same bed.

This was fine with Coyote because she hated sleeping in anything but a nice cot with a fresh fluffy.

If Coyote was queen of the fluffies, Snuggles was queen of the cots, laying claim to more beds than she could possibly sleep in. This tended to annoy everyone except Sargeant, Gina, and Sampson, who only wanted one bed between them since they insisted on doing everything together, including sleeping on the same cot.

Higgins thought everyone was altogether too comfortable at Old Friends. "Cots and fluffies," he grumbled to Sebastian. "In the old days, you were lucky even to have a doghouse. Why, when I first arrived here, you just slept in the sand. There wasn't an Old Friends home. There weren't even any octagons. You're all too spoiled. I remember when . . ."

Higgins liked to go on about the old days, but the other dogs paid little attention to all his stories of legendary heroes, founding dogfathers, golden biscuits, and the Federal Reserve Tree. After all, for most dogs, it's today that matters, not what happened yesterday, or last year, or what might happen tomorrow. There were always exciting new rescue stories, new dogs to meet and greet, and fond farewells to dogs being adopted.

Today, for example, the hot gossip was about a new arrival, Peppermint Patty, who arrived at Best Friends a few days before after spending five long years living underground.

Peppermint Patty and Duke

"Come on out into the sunshine one more time," said Buck to his new friend, Peppermint Patty. "It's nice outside once you get used to it and the fresh air will do you good."

Peppermint Patty peeked through the door again. She still wasn't sure about coming out. It certainly looked nice out there in the sun. But it was scary, too, because until she arrived at Dogtown, she'd completely forgotten what sunlight was.

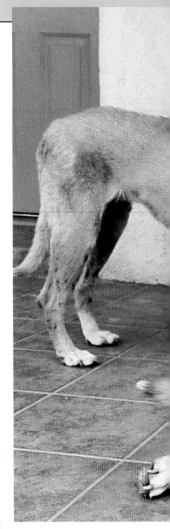

Peppermint Patty had spent the past five years living alone in the basement of a big-city kennel. All that time, she'd never seen the light of day. So, it was going to take her a little time getting used to the idea of being a real dog and playing with the other dogs out in the sunshine.

Buck was being very patient with her. This spry twenty-year-old arrived at Dogtown the same day she did. He'd had a good life, but then for some reason he couldn't understand, he'd been dropped off at an animal hospital, and nobody ever came back to collect him.

"Come on out," he urged one more time, and, yes, slowly and cautiously she followed him outdoors and sat blinking in the sunlight. Somebody gave her a big hug, and she wagged her tail. Still, it was a bit overwhelming and after a few minutes, she trotted back indoors. Tomorrow she would go out again and stay out a bit longer.

As Peppermint Patty came back in, Higgins gave her a good sniffing all over. Then he wandered back to Sebastian. "Five years underground is not that big a deal," he grumbled to the other dogs. "Why, when I first came here, there was a dog who hadn't even . . ."

As the day ended, the dogs all settled down on their cots and fluffies for a nice evening snooze. Sebastian grinned and nodded off, dreaming about birthdays and carrot cake.

Peppermint Patty (left) followed her new friend, Buck, outdoors.

Oneida, a special favorite at Old Friends, likes to dance at dinnertime.

<u>Epilog</u>:

A Perfect Day to Count
the Tennis Balls

There hadn't been many tennis balls to count this afternoon, but Ginger enjoyed it nonetheless. Dogtown was humming, and she still liked to play her part, even though she'd gotten more than a little creaky herself.

Although she would have been very welcome, Ginger had never moved into Old Friends. The Chesapeake Bay was her home, so she and Higgins lived at either end of Dogtown. They were the last of the old gang—the end of a generation. The Sheriff, the Dogfather, and her other old pals had all gone over the Rainbow Bridge. She'd even outlasted her own pups, who had gone the same way a couple of years ago. She'd be ready to join them all soon. And so would Higgins, for sure. Meanwhile, two nice black mutts, Butterfly and Francesca, had moved in with her at the Chesapeake Bay, but they preferred chasing the breakfast truck to collecting the tennis balls.

Old friends meet old friends at Old Friends.

Still, the Federal Reserve Tree was as shady as ever and visitors to Dogtown loved to help out by picking up tennis balls and lost treats and bringing them there. Ginger appreciated that, but she still enjoyed going out occasionally to do the rounds herself.

All over Dogtown, new octagons were replacing the old homes. There was a whole new suburb being built—Dogtown Heights—for dogs that need special care. Ginger liked the new world that was growing up around her and all the new faces—the rowdy gangs of young strays, the maternity center that had taken the place of Suzy's old kindergarten, and the notorious Little Dogs encampment, ruled over by the infamous mobster, Brownie the Dachshund.

And she especially liked Mayor Jethro. He did such a fine job of stepping into the Sheriff's paws as host of Dogtown. Why, he was quite an old guy

Brownie (center), the infamous mobster of Little Dogs, with some of his gang.

Rupert rests his chin on a low wall overlooking Dogtown.

A perfect day to count the tennis balls.

himself these days.

On her way back to the Federal Reserve Tree, Ginger picked up a tennis ball or two and watched a group of new dogs arriving at the sanctuary and looking up at the huge sky, just as she had done all those years ago. Soon they'd be learning their manners from the older dogs, getting their act together, and then mostly moving on to good new homes.

"Just keep the tennis balls circulating," she thought to herself as she dropped one more onto the pile and went indoors for a nice evening snooze.